Who Was
Levi Strauss?

by Ellen Labrecque

illustrated by Stephen Marchesi

Penguin Workshop

For my mom, Marge Cosgrove,
who worked for the Levi Strauss company—EL

For my friend and agent Janet at Storybook Arts,
thirty years on—SM

PENGUIN WORKSHOP
An Imprint of Penguin Random House LLC, New York

Visit us online at www.penguinrandomhouse.com.

Library of Congress Cataloging-in-Publication Data is available upon request.

ISBN 9780448488561 (paperback)   10 9 8 7 6 5 4 3 2 1
ISBN 9780593224601 (library binding)   10 9 8 7 6 5 4 3 2 1

Contents

Who Was Levi Strauss?

On March 14, 1853, Levi Strauss stepped off a steamship and onto a dock in San Francisco. At that time, most of California was still wild and untamed. But San Francisco was growing fast. Levi was one of thirty-four thousand immigrants to arrive by ship that year. The city was bustling. Theaters, saloons, and supply stores lined the walkways leading to the waterfront. The air smelled of salt and fish from the ocean. Sounds of ship horns blasted through the streets, as people crowded around the docks to buy everything from food to lumber and steel.

Back in New York, Levi had sold clothes and sewing materials with his brothers at J. Strauss & Brother. But now, he set his sights farther, wider. He was coming to California to expand his business.

When he arrived, Levi looked like the other businessmen. He stood five feet six inches tall, had dark hair and a big beard. He wore black pants, a black vest, jacket, and a bow tie—the style most businessmen wore at the time. Levi blended in with the crowd.

Why were so many people flocking to San Francisco? Gold had been discovered in California in 1848. People were racing west to try to make their fortune. Levi, though, wasn't one of these gold seekers. Instead, Levi knew gold miners needed sturdy clothes—especially pants—to wear while they worked in the dusty riverbeds. Levi planned to sell them rugged, long-lasting pants, but he didn't know how in-demand they would become.

Levi's jeans first became very popular with miners, but today nearly everybody wears them.

More than one billion pairs of jeans are sold around the world every year. They are still made in a similar style, with the same denim material used so long ago. The pants that Levi Strauss made for workingmen are still a fashion favorite today!

CHAPTER 1
Life in Bavaria

Levi Strauss was born Loeb Strauss on February 26, 1829, in Buttenheim, Bavaria. His parents were Hirsch and Rebecca Strauss. Loeb was the youngest of seven children. Five of them were from his father's first marriage. Hirsch was a hardworking door-to-door salesman, who sold sewing supplies such as fabric, thread, and buttons.

Rebecca stayed at home and took care of the children. The Strauss family lived in a cramped space on the first floor of a house that only had a large living room, a kitchen, and one bedroom.

The Strauss family was a close and loving one. The children were taught to help and look out

for one another. The family was Jewish. Loeb's childhood was filled with going to Hebrew School (a school for Jewish children), helping his mother with chores, and playing with his brothers and sisters and his cousins, who also lived in the same town.

Bavaria

Bavarian flag

Bavaria is one of the sixteen states of Germany. It has a population of more than twelve million, and is located in the southeastern part of the country. In the 1800s, Bavaria was a kingdom in the Germanic Confederation (what Germany was called at the time). When Loeb was born, it was ruled by King Ludwig I and about four million people lived there.

Bavaria's capital city is Munich. It is Germany's third-largest city. In September or October, Munich hosts a giant fair called Oktoberfest that lasts sixteen to eighteen days. People come from all over the world to drink and eat, ride on amusement rides, play games, and listen to music. The city has been hosting a festival like this almost every fall since 1810.

Most people in Bavaria were Roman Catholic, but the Strausses were Jewish. Many people there hated Loeb's family and other Jewish people *just* because of their religion.

Government rules made life even worse for the Strauss family and all Jewish people there. They were told where they had to live and where they could work. Jewish people were not allowed to vote, and had to pay more taxes to the government than non-Jewish citizens. No matter how much money Hirsch made, the government took a lot of it.

In 1840, when Loeb was eleven, his older brother Jonathan moved to New York City. Another older brother, Lippmann, followed in 1841. People from all over Europe were coming to New York at this time. The city was bustling with jobs and opportunities. New York offered lots of different ways for people to make a living. In 1824 the Erie Canal had opened. The canal was a 363-mile waterway that connected the Hudson River to Lake Erie. This made it much easier to get goods to people living in America's Midwest. This meant

New York manufacturers could make things such as clothing and furniture and ship them out to the middle of the country. As a result, new New York businesses were popping up every day.

And the Strauss brothers wanted to open a business, too.

Soon after Lippmann joined Jonathan in the United States, they opened a small store in New York City called J. Strauss & Brother. They sold sewing supplies, but unlike their father, they didn't have to travel at all. They had a store, and customers came to them instead.

In fact, the Strauss brothers called themselves store-princes. They felt rich and royal compared to the way traveling salesmen worked.

Back in Bavaria, Loeb saw how difficult the job was for his father, especially carrying his things—which could weigh as much as seventy pounds—in a bag on his back. The work made his father weak and sick. In 1846, when Loeb was seventeen, Hirsch died from tuberculosis,

a disease that affects the lungs. The Strauss family had struggled to make enough money when Hirsch was alive. Now, they struggled even more.

Loeb was worried about his family, and especially about his mother. He felt like no matter how hard they worked, they could never make ends meet. He wanted to work hard like his father. But Loeb also wanted to work hard in a place where his efforts would be rewarded.

At this time, "America fever" was spreading throughout the Jewish population in Bavaria. Everybody wanted to go to America. They thought they had a much better chance to make money in America than they ever could in Bavaria. They wanted a better life. Thousands of Bavarian Jewish people had already fled their country. The Strauss family decided it was time to move to America, too. At this time,

Loeb's mother had to ask permission from the Bavarian government to leave. She couldn't leave without asking them first. In a letter to the government, Rebecca wrote: "My sons who are located in America have landed on their feet.

For, according to their letters, they are successfully engaged in business. I have therefore decided to emigrate with my remaining children to seek my goal in that other part of the world."

It took more than a year, but the Strauss family was finally granted permission to leave Bavaria. They were coming to America to make better lives for themselves.

CHAPTER 2
Coming to America

Loeb, his mother, and two of his sisters, Voegela and Maila, set sail to America in the winter of 1848. Loeb was nineteen years old. The trip took several weeks. They traveled in the lower decks of the ship. This was the only kind of ticket poor people could afford. But this made the trip very hard. The ocean waves felt rough, especially from the lower decks. Many people suffered seasickness. There was not enough food to eat or water to drink. People in these lower decks—called steerage—never bathed during the voyage. By the end of the trip, the whole ship smelled of filth and rotten food. Some people died of disease during the journey.

After many weeks, the ship arrived in
New York City. The passengers disembarked
on the East Side of Manhattan. The
docks were loud, crowded, and busy.
Ships were arriving from all over the world
with immigrants and goods such as fabric,
lumber, and coal. People were buying and
selling clothes, furniture, and even musical

instruments all day and night along the docks.
Not far from the docks, new buildings were
being built. There were markets filled with
meat and cheeses, and brand-new stores like
the one Loeb's brothers had opened to sell
fabric. The Strauss family was tired from their
difficult journey, but felt lucky to have reached
their new home.

The family moved in with Jonathan and Lippmann, sharing their small New York apartment, called a tenement.

Loeb went to work with his brothers at the family store in the same neighborhood as their apartment on the Lower East Side. The three brothers worked long hours buying and selling dry goods, items like coats, pants, hats, buttons, thread, and fabric to make clothes. Loeb was now known by his Hebrew name, Levi. Levi sounded more American, and was easier to pronounce for non-German-speaking people who came to shop at the store. Levi's brothers and sisters also changed their names. Jonathan was now called Jonas, and Lippmann was called Louis. Voegela was now Fanny, and Maila became known as Mary.

Life in New York was better for Levi than it had been in Bavaria. The family was reunited.

Tenement Living

During the entire nineteenth century, immigrants flocked to New York City. They were looking for a better life than they had in their own countries. So many people came, in fact, that there were not enough places for them to live once they arrived. To solve this problem, many low-rise, four-story buildings on the Lower East Side of the city were turned into six to eight apartments, called tenements.

Many families who lived in tenements faced terrible living conditions. These cramped apartments were often made from cheap materials and had little to no indoor plumbing. And because of poor ventilation, tenements also had bad air quality. This resulted in disasters like fires, and left people at risk of catching many diseases that spread rapidly.

By 1900, 70 percent of New York's entire population (more than two million people) lived in tenement housing. Laws were eventually passed to make tenements safer places to live.

They had enough to eat. Their neighborhood was called *Kleindeutchland* (Little Germany) because so many German immigrants had settled there. Unlike in Germany, however, the US government didn't tell Jewish people, or other immigrant groups, where they could live. They were free.

CHAPTER 3
California, Here I Come

On January 31, 1853, Levi, who was now almost twenty-four years old, became an American citizen. He had been in the country for almost six years. Now that he was a citizen, Levi was ready to explore the West. Gold had recently been discovered in California, and many people began to travel there with the hope of finding their own fortunes.

The California Gold Rush (1848–1855)

James Marshall

The California Gold Rush began on January 24, 1848, when carpenter James Marshall discovered gold in the American River, a hundred miles inland from the city of San Francisco. Newspapers across the country ran stories about the discovery. Before the gold was found, only about one thousand settlers lived in the area. By the end of 1849, more than one hundred thousand settlers lived there!

The people who came, mostly men, traveled thousands of miles to get to California. Their trips were difficult and dangerous. Once they arrived, many lived in tents along the river, digging for gold with just a pick and a shovel. It was estimated that more than 750,000 pounds of gold—worth $2 billion— was found during the Gold Rush. But there were a lot of people that were looking for this treasure. Some miners made as much as a hundred dollars a day; the average was twenty dollars a day. Often, they would find nothing at all, which meant they didn't make any money. Gold digging was hard work, the hours were long, and the cost of living—clothes, food, and shelter—was high. The people who made the most money during the Gold Rush were the businessmen who sold supplies, food, and clothes to the miners— not the miners themselves.

Levi wanted to go to California, too. But it wasn't to dig for gold. Levi and his brothers knew that miners needed sturdy clothes to live and work there. The Strauss brothers saw an opportunity. There were already many fabric stores in New York. But in San Francisco, theirs would be one of only a few.

In February 1853, Levi decided to leave New York for California. He was young and single. This made it easier for him to head out on his own. He had a couple of different travel options, but none of them were easy. In the end, Levi

chose not to travel overland. He would take a ship—but with a shortcut.

Levi boarded a US Mail steamship headed south to the country of Panama in Central America. This trip took only about ten days. Levi then crossed the narrow strip of land called the Isthmus of Panama, which is only about fifty miles wide, to get to the Pacific Ocean.

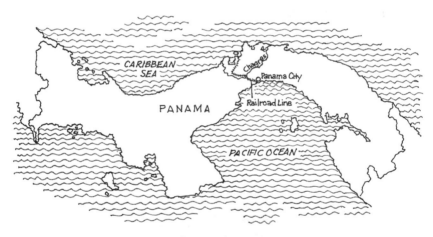

Isthmus of Panama

In order to cross the country, Levi took the Panama Railway, then a canoe up the Chagres River. He then rented a mule for the final twenty miles of the journey to Panama City. There, he boarded a steamer to San Francisco. Levi sailed into San Francisco Bay on March 14, 1853. The whole trip took him just over a month.

SAN FRANCISCO

CALIFORNIA

San Francisco is a city located midway along the coast of California. From there it is about a hundred miles inland to the American River, where the first gold had been found. Thanks to the Gold Rush, more than one hundred thousand non-native people lived there at the time of Levi's arrival.

The city was booming with activity, especially along the docks. The smell of salt water from the bay swirled in the air. Crowds of people loaded and unloaded cargo from ships. Others picked up their mail or greeted passengers who were arriving for the first time.

Levi, along with everybody else, depended on the ships to bring everything they needed—from food, to clothing, to building supplies.

San Francisco was a rapidly growing city. It was growing so fast, in fact, it was called "an instant city." The year Levi stepped off the ship, the city had one hundred and sixty hotels, sixty-six restaurants, sixty-three bakeries, and nineteen banks! Less than six years earlier, this same area had been practically empty and desert-like!

A couple of weeks after Levi reached San Francisco, he received many boxes from his brothers. They were filled with silk and canvas cloth for Levi to sell. Look out, California—the Strauss family was open for business!

CHAPTER 4
A Natural Salesman

With the items his brothers sent him, Levi opened a wholesale dry goods warehouse. *Dry goods* is a phrase used to describe clothing such as coats, pants, shirts, hats, as well as tools to make clothing such as needles and thread. These are different from other goods such as food and building materials. Levi named the new business Levi Strauss & Company. Like many other businesses, his warehouse was located right near the waterfront. In order to protect it from high tides, it was built on pilings or wood poles.

Levi sold fabric, bedding, and sewing supplies to local merchants, who in turn sold them directly to customers. Most people who came to California arrived with as little as possible.

Their journey was too hard and long to bring a lot of stuff with them. Instead, they bought the goods when they arrived. Many of Levi's customers were miners, who sometimes paid Levi in gold for his merchandise.

Levi's supplies became very popular. At times, Levi ran out of the supplies his brothers sent him before a new shipment arrived. Levi went down to the waterfront and waited for other ships filled with cargo to be delivered. Some of the cargo was sold to the person willing to pay the highest price. Levi knew he would make his money back, plus a little more, once he sold the merchandise to the stores.

Most items were more expensive to buy in San Francisco than in New York. People were willing to pay a higher price because things were harder to find, since California was still mostly wilderness. It only became a state in 1850 after the Mexican-American War.

As more people arrived to California, some dishonest businessmen sold miners maps with

fake places where they could
find gold, or digging
tools that didn't work or
broke easily.

Levi, though, was honest.
He remembered how unfairly his family had
been treated in Bavaria. He didn't want to do that
to anybody else. He always tried to make sure
his products were of the best quality.

Merchants often liked to buy from Levi
because he was known to be very trustworthy.

The Mexican-American War (1846–1848)

The war between the United States and Mexico was a fight for land. While much of the West belonged to Mexico (including the southern parts of California), President James Polk and many citizens

of the United States believed in manifest destiny, the idea that God wanted the United States to stretch from the Atlantic Ocean on the East Coast to the Pacific Ocean on the West Coast. Mexico believed it owned the land west of

President James Polk

the Nueces River in Texas. The United States said it owned the land all the way up to the Rio Grande, which is about one hundred miles farther west than the Nueces.

The United States declared war on Mexico on May 13, 1846, and the United States won every battle. The fighting ended on September 14, 1847, when the United States took over Mexico City, the country's capital. In the treaty signed on February 2, 1848, Mexico surrendered and gave the United States the land that today includes the states of Texas, New Mexico, Utah, Nevada, Arizona, western Colorado, and California.

He also had a variety of good supplies his brothers sent him from New York and he never charged too much. This meant Levi had many repeat customers. Soon he was making a lot of money from his sales. In July 1855, Levi shipped gold back to his brothers in New York for the first time. The gold was worth more than $10,000 (it would be worth about $250,000 today).

Levi kept sending money the rest of the year. In total for 1855, Levi sent more than $80,000 back east ($2 million today). Levi's brothers back in New York changed the name of their company from J. Strauss & Brother to J. Strauss Brother & Company. But in California, Levi was building his own name for himself.

CHAPTER 5
The West Opens Up

In 1855, Levi's sister Fanny, her husband, David Stern, and their children, Jacob and Caroline, joined Levi in San Francisco from New York. Levi's business continued to expand, and David

could help him run it. Levi's brother Louis moved to San Francisco a year later. Jonas remained in New York selling dry goods as well as sending shipments to Levi in San Francisco. Over the

David Stern

next couple of years, Levi's profits grew and grew. In addition to being reliable, Levi was especially good at making friends. He enjoyed talking and meeting new folks.

When Levi first moved west, letters sent by ship or by a stagecoach took months to arrive.

Supplies took even longer. But in April 1860, a mail service called the Pony Express helped Levi get a letter to New York in just two weeks, which helped him reach his brother back East, and to get supplies shipped more quickly, too.

Levi spent all his time working in his business. He didn't have a wife, and instead, lived with his sister Fanny and her family. While Levi and David ran the family business, Fanny did everything for her brother, including cooking, cleaning, and laundry.

Levi's sister, Fanny Stern

The Pony Express (1860–1861)

The Pony Express (officially called the Central Overland California & Pike's Peak Express Company) was a horse-and-rider mail delivery system between St. Joseph, Missouri, and Sacramento, California. (A train took the rest of the mail from Missouri to New York, and a steamship took the mail from Sacramento to San Francisco.)

Galloping at speeds of up to 25 miles per hour, each rider covered seventy-five to a hundred miles each day, changing horses every ten to fifteen miles. Then, at one of some 190 relay stations across the West, a new rider

grabbed a twenty-pound bag of mail and took off quickly.

The Pony Express operated for eighteen months and delivered 34,753 letters. It stopped operating when the transcontinental telegraph, a system that used electricity to send coded messages through wires, was completed in 1861.

CHAPTER 6
Merchant Prince of the Pacific Coast

Levi Strauss & Company kept growing. They began selling their goods to stores not just in San Francisco, but all over the West.

In local newspapers, Levi was called one of the "Merchant Princes of the Pacific Coast." People around town began to recognize him in the street. When he ate in restaurants, people whispered that Levi Strauss was there.

But Levi remained a man of the people. He always asked his employees to call him Levi, not Mr. Strauss.

He also helped the San Francisco community any time he could. Levi had joined a synagogue soon after he arrived. Many Jewish people like Levi had come to California from all over the world to make their fortune. This meant Levi had a ready, built-in community with people who practiced the same faith. Levi received help and advice from more experienced Jewish businessmen who had arrived before him.

Levi gave money to help build Emanu-El synagogue, a place for Jewish people to worship. It was important for Levi to have a public place for the Jewish

Temple Emanu-El

people of San Francisco to pray. Levi believed in *tzedakah*, the Jewish practice of helping people in need. He also joined an organization that supported Jewish widows and their families. He gave money to orphanages and schools in the area. Levi especially liked helping young children. He knew they represented the future of San Francisco, and he wanted his adopted city to prosper.

While Levi filled his daily life in California with business and charity work, things were different in other parts of the country. In 1861, the American Civil War broke out.

The Civil War was not fought on California soil. But most of the people there, including Levi, supported the Union and President Abraham Lincoln. During the fighting, Levi's company donated thousands of dollars to the Sanitary Commission, which helped care for sick and wounded Union soldiers. Levi was a proud citizen of the United States. He wanted his country to remain united. This didn't mean he forgot his immigrant roots. Levi was also a member of the California Immigrant Union. This was a group that encouraged immigrants from Europe and the East Coast to move to California. Levi and this group were thrilled when the Transcontinental Railroad was completed in 1869. The cross-country railroad allowed trains to travel from New York to California, which made it easier for people and goods to travel than ever before.

The Civil War (1861–1865)

The American Civil War was fought between Northern states (the Union) and Southern states (the Confederacy). Seven Southern states formed their own country after Abraham Lincoln was elected president in 1860 because they were against abolishing slavery; four more states joined them later. For four years, the North and South fought bloody battles. More than six hundred thousand soldiers died. The South eventually surrendered on April 9, 1865. The Thirteenth Amendment, which outlawed slavery, was added to the US Constitution that same year.

Through the years, ships with Levi's gold on
them had been lost at sea. One ship was caught
in a storm, causing it to sink to the bottom of
the ocean. Another time a ship caught fire,
causing most of the passengers aboard to die

and all the cargo to be destroyed. Levi and other
businessmen knew the trains would be faster, but
they also hoped they would be safer.

Transcendental Railroad

The Transcontinental Railroad was the first railroad track to run all the way from New York to California. Tracks had already existed from New York to Council Bluffs, Iowa. But in 1863, a railroad company began building a new line toward the

east from Sacramento, California, while another company began building tracks west. Thousands of workers, mainly Chinese immigrants, did the hard work of laying down the rails. The two teams finally met on May 10, 1869, in Promontory, Utah. The new tracks covered 1,800 miles and took six years to build. People could now reach California from New York in just two weeks' time.

CHAPTER 7
The Birth of Blue Jeans

Levi Strauss & Company was now in headquarters that included a huge showroom in San Francisco's business district. Buyers visited 14-16 Battery Street and looked at the products before buying them. Levi was now selling men's

and women's clothing that was made in a New York factory, then shipped to California. He also sold blankets, fabrics, and children's clothes.

In July 1872, Levi received a letter that would change his life forever. The letter was from one of his customers—Jacob Davis, a tailor in Reno, Nevada. Jacob bought denim cloth from Levi to make pants. Denim was a strong cotton fabric, also called serge, made in Nîmes, France. (In fact, the word *denim* means "from Nîmes.") Jacob made denim pants for miners in the Reno area. Workers out West had been complaining that their pants did not last. The pockets ripped off easily—especially when they put their tools in them. The seams were not strong enough. In the letter to Levi, Jacob explained how he solved this problem. He put in tiny metal pins called rivets around the pockets and the front seams. This helped keep the pants from ripping. Nobody had ever thought to secure the pockets like this.

Davis wrote that these pants were extremely popular because they were so long-lasting. All the miners and workers wanted them. Jacob worked by himself, sewing the pants alone. "I found the demand so large that I cannot make them up fast enough," he wrote. Jacob needed Levi's help to manufacture more of them quicker.

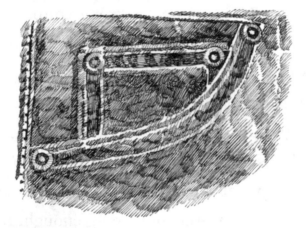

Metal rivets on the pocket of Levi's work pants

Jacob also explained that he wanted to apply for a patent for the riveted pants. A patent is the legal right of a person to sell an idea for a certain number of years. This means nobody else can use the idea and make money from it. Jacob didn't have the money for the patent application. He knew Levi did. Jacob also knew he could trust Levi not to steal his idea. He asked Levi to help him apply for the patent, and then help him make more of these pants.

Levi was a smart businessman. He knew a good idea when he saw one. He agreed to help Jacob. On May 20, 1873, the US Patent Office granted Levi and Jacob patent number 139,121 for an "Improvement in Fastening Pocket-Openings" on men's work pants. It was on this day that blue jeans were officially born.

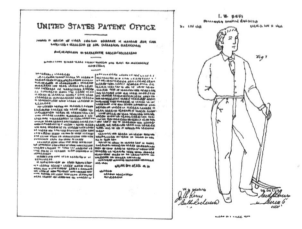

Jacob Davis (1831–1908)

Jacob Davis was born Jacob Youphes in Riga, Latvia, which was then part of the Russian Empire. In 1854, at the age of twenty-three, he immigrated to New York. When he arrived, he changed his last name to Davis to sound more American. Jacob first worked in New York as a tailor. Silver had been discovered in Nevada in 1859, and Jacob moved there to make clothes for miners. In 1868, another silver discovery was made, and Davis soon owned a tailor shop on the main street in Reno.

It was there that he made a pair of riveted pants for a laborer who wanted pockets strong enough to hold his tools. After working with Levi Strauss to secure a patent, Jacob and his family moved to San Francisco. He lived there for the rest of his life, overseeing the manufacture of pants that would change the world—Levi's jeans.

CHAPTER 8
Blue Jean Fever

Levi opened a factory to make these new pants. It was just a couple blocks from Levi's showroom and offices. Jacob moved to San Francisco to be the plant's head tailor and floor manager. Levi had never made things before. He was used to having finished clothes shipped from New York. This was a new challenge, but Levi was ready. He bought machines and hired fifty sewing machine operators to work them. In addition to the jeans, Levi and Jacob also produced jackets with the riveted pockets.

Although the denim fabric first came from France, manufacturers now began making this material in the United States. The material for Levi's jeans came from a plant in Manchester,

New Hampshire. The first pairs had two front pockets and one back pocket. There were buttons around the waist for suspenders to hook. Like he always did, Levi picked the best type of material on the market, XX Denim. In the clothing world, the XX meant the material was extra, extra strong.

The material Levi used was durable and meant for people with dirty and difficult jobs, like miners. At the time, it was the heaviest clothing fabric milled.

The original fabric for Levi's pants was white. Levi could have dyed the pants any color he wanted. But Jacob and Levi chose blue, because indigo, the plant used to dye clothes blue, was grown right in California. They used orange thread to stitch the seams. The color matched the rivets. With this orange stitching, Jacob sewed two curving "V's" on the back pocket of each pair of jeans. The V's looked like the wings of an eagle,

Present-day Levi's trademark symbol

the national bird of the United States. In fact, Levi's "wings" are the oldest clothing trademark symbol still in use today. A business's trademark is like a person's signature. Only the business that owns the trademark is allowed to use it. It identifies who they are.

Levi's pants were always made to fit big and long on his customers. He knew this material would shrink when it became wet. He never wanted them to become too tight or small after they were washed.

The rivets were tricky to apply to the pants. As a result, the overalls required more labor time and were more expensive to make than other pants. This meant they had to be sold at a higher price, too. Levi's new overalls were sold at about two dollars a pair, while other pants were sold for fifty cents! Despite the high price, miners, cowboys, and lumberjacks still wanted them. They were made to last. Levi began advertising his pants in newspapers across the country. The ads read, "To the workingman, mechanic, drayman and miner. Buy Levi Strauss &

Company's celebrated Patented Riveted Duck and Denim Overalls."

Thanks to these advertisements and word of mouth, storekeepers around the West began to buy Levi's pants to resell in other places. Levi's brother Jonas soon opened a manufacturing plant in New York to make these riveted pants and sell them there. Now these sought-after work pants were much more widely available.

Why "Jeans"?

When Levi first began making jeans, they were called waist-high overalls. Laborers and farmers typically wore overalls. Calling his new pants a type of overalls helped buyers understand exactly what he was selling.

Levi used a denim material for the pants. But he also used a similar type of fabric originally made in Genoa, Italy. The French word for Genoa is Genes. As time went on, the French word Genes was changed to the American word jeans.

Levi's pants were called waist-high overalls until the 1950s. By then, teenagers were wearing these pants, too. They decided to call the product "jeans," perhaps because they thought it sounded cooler. By 1960, Levi Strauss & Company decided to officially change the name.

Genoa

ITALY

By the end of 1873, Levi had sold over 21,000 riveted pants and jackets. A year later, Levi had sold 70,500 pieces of riveted clothing. Other companies tried to sell riveted pants like the ones Levi was selling, but they could not. Levi and Jacob owned the patent, so they were the only ones allowed to sell them for now. On October 11, 1874, an article ran in the *New York Times* titled "San Francisco Millionaires." Levi was one of the fifty men on this list. But Levi's company was worth even more.

While Levi enjoyed his wealth and jean success, he had to deal with a personal loss. David Stern, his brother-in-law, died on January 2, 1874. He was fifty-one. David and Fanny had seven children. David had been one of Levi's business partners and a good friend for many years. Fanny and David's oldest son, Jacob, now twenty-three, took over his father's position in the company.

Levi's sister Mary had also died, back in New York. Mary and her husband, William Sahlein, had helped Levi run the company from the East

Coast. After Mary's death, William and his three children moved to California to join Levi.

In 1875, Fanny and William married each other. Fanny and her seven children, and William and his three children, all moved in together.

Levi and his brother Louis lived with them, too! All fourteen of them moved to 621 Leavenworth Street in the heart of San Francisco. It was a beautiful mansion where everybody had plenty of space. Levi enjoyed spending time with his nieces and nephews. He treated them like they were his own children.

And his business grew even bigger. The company now made a line of denim work shirts in addition to the jeans. They also began selling their clothes all over the world—from Texas and Canada, to as far away as France. The pants were comfortable, simple, and most importantly, durable. Workers around the world wanted a pair of Levi's jeans.

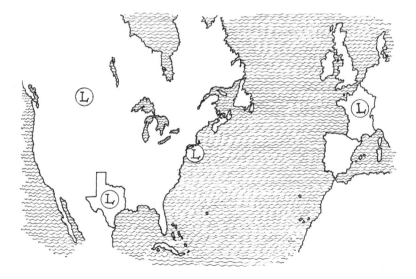

CHAPTER 9
Levi's Workers

The more pants Levi sold, the more he had to make. Levi needed to hire workers—a lot of workers—to fill this demand. It wasn't hard to find people to do these jobs—it was just tricky to find the workers Levi wanted.

In 1877, Chinese immigrants made up one fifth of the workforce in California. This meant that for every one hundred workers, twenty of them were Chinese. And all these folks were willing to work for lower pay than white people. This made the white workers angry, which resulted in the passage of the Chinese Exclusion Act.

Chinese Exclusion Act (1882–1943)

In 1882, the United States government passed a law that stopped Chinese immigrants from entering the country. The law also prevented Chinese people who had been in the country and left from returning. This exclusion act was the first law that turned the United States from being a welcoming country for all immigrants to only accepting some people.

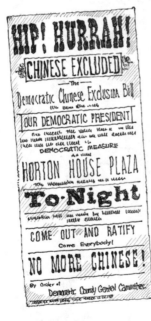

The law was repealed in 1943.

Levi pledged not to hire Chinese immigrants. At the time, this seemed to make good business sense to him. His customers were mostly white workers. He thought they would buy his clothes over others because he didn't hire Chinese immigrants. Levi's decision to not hire Chinese immigrants was an act of discrimination— not treating a group of people fairly based on their race. Levi treated Chinese workers the same way Jewish people had been treated in Bavaria.

Even though he didn't hire Chinese workers, Levi still found plenty of people to make his pants. By the early 1880s, he had close to three hundred employees, including factory workers, salesmen, and bookkeepers. His sales reached over $2 million.

But Levi and Jacob's patent was set to run out in 1890. This meant other companies could soon start selling riveted pants, too.

Levi wanted to make sure his jeans stood out once other riveted pants appeared in stores. Levi put a brown leather patch on the back of every pair. The patch showed two horses facing away from each other. Each horse is tied to the same pair of jeans. The horses pull in the opposite direction, but the jeans refuse to rip.

Levi used a picture, not words, on this logo. A lot of his customers could not read. He wanted to make sure everybody understood the message: Levi's jeans are so tough, even powerful animals can't rip them. Levi had flyers printed up with this logo for salesmen to carry. Underneath the design, it said "It's No Use They Can't Be Ripped."

Levi's pants were now known as the "Two Horse Brand." Levi Strauss & Company still uses this logo today.

CHAPTER 10
Sharing the Wealth

Levi made his nephews, Jacob, Sigmund, Louis, and Abraham, partners in his company in 1890. David and Fanny's sons had grown up working for their uncle; now they were rising leaders. This also made it clear the nephews would continue to run the company after Levi died.

Around the same time, Levi's XX jeans were renamed 501. Although no one is sure why this number was chosen, the numeral "5" always meant the highest-quality products to Levi. These 501 jeans became Levi's most popular item.

(They continue to be a best seller and are now called "Levi's Legendary 501 Jeans.")

In 1895, Levi turned sixty-six years old. He had earned several million dollars over his lifetime. But since he never married and had his own children, his business was his life.

"I am a bachelor," he told a reporter. "I don't believe that a man who once forms the habit of being busy can retire and be contented . . . My happiness lies in my routine work."

Two years later, Levi showed how much he still enjoyed working by agreeing to allow his image to appear on a funny advertisement for his company. On the flyer, Levi is shown wearing a pair of the

jeans and climbing a fence. A scary-looking dog is biting on the waistband of his jeans. The caption of the flyer reads: "Never Rip, Never Tear, Wish They Did Now."

The especially funny part was that Levi probably never wore jeans in his life. He was a businessman and always wore suits. But he was willing to laugh at himself.

In 1897, Levi donated enough money to fund twenty-eight scholarships at the University of

California, Berkeley. The money was awarded to poor students who couldn't afford tuition. He also gave money to a cemetery back in Buttenheim, Bavaria. It was the cemetery where his father, Hirsch, was buried.

University of California campus, 1897

In 1902, Levi was seventy-three and spent most of his time with his extended family. On September 26, he had dinner with his nephew Jacob and his family. Levi went to bed that evening, and died in his sleep. The entire city of San Francisco grieved. Flags in the business district flew at half-mast to honor him, and articles in the newspaper praised Levi for his good deeds in the city, his compassion, and his extremely successful business.

After a quiet but crowded ceremony at the house on Leavenworth Street, Levi was buried in Hills of Eternity Memorial Park, a Jewish cemetery in nearby Colma. On the day of the funeral, businesses in the city shut down. San Francisco wanted to show respect for one of its most honored and beloved citizens.

And Levi loved the city right back. In his

will, Levi left thousands of dollars to orphanages and old-age homes, and millions to his family. Meanwhile, his four nephews continued to run the business as planned.

CHAPTER 11
The Levi Legacy

Over the next four years, Levi's company grew under his nephews' leadership. But on April 18, 1906, an earthquake hit San Francisco. The Levi Strauss & Company building and its factories were damaged or destroyed, along with the rest of the city.

1906 San Francisco Earthquake

An earthquake struck San Francisco at 5:12 a.m. on April 18, 1906. The size of earthquakes is ranked on a point scale called the Richter Scale. This one was ranked 7.9. People who survived the quake that day described it sounding like the "roar of ten thousand lions."

Fires broke out all over the city because of burst gas pipes. The fire burned for four days until it was finally put out by rain. The fire destroyed more than five hundred blocks in the city, which included

twenty-eight thousand buildings. More than three thousand people died and more than two hundred and fifty thousand were left homeless. People were forced to camp in parks around the city. It was one of the worst natural disasters in United States history. When the city was finally rebuilt, most of the buildings were constructed to be fire- and earthquake-resistant.

While many of Levi's important papers about the history of the company were destroyed in the

earthquake, Levi's nephews got the company up and running again in no time. On April 27, less than ten days after the quake, they put an ad in the newspaper reassuring customers that "they will positively resume business."

The men set up temporary offices in Oakland, just outside San Francisco, while they rebuilt. Their new headquarters on 98 Battery Street in San Francisco was completed by 1908.

By the 1920s, Levi's jeans were the top men's work pants in the Western United States. But the company started to notice something. People were calling jeans, any jeans, Levi's, even if Levi's didn't make them. In 1928, the company obtained a trademark for the name "Levi's."

Then, to make their jeans even more special, they created a red fabric tab with the word "Levi's" printed on it. They sewed the tab—like a tiny ribbon— on the outside of the right back pocket. Now everybody knew which jeans were Levi's and which were not.

Movies also helped make Levi's popular with everybody, not just workers. In the 1939 movie *Stagecoach*, an actor named John Wayne wore a pair of 501 jeans. The movie made a big star of John Wayne, and also a star of Levi's.

John Wayne in *Stagecoach*

In the 1940s, Levi's took advantage of the jeans' rising popularity. They ran an ad that showed a boy in Levi's walking with books in his hand. The words on the ad read, "Levi's: Right for School!" At this time, boys wore dress pants and girls wore dresses to school. They did not wear jeans. But Levi's advertisement helped change this. Kids could look cool like the movie stars, even if they were just going to school.

In the decades that followed, cool rebels, played by actors like Marlon Brando in the 1953 movie *The Wild One*, also began wearing Levi's in films. In 1957, singer Elvis Presley wore jeans in a rock and roll film called *Jailhouse Rock*.

Elvis Presley in *Jailhouse Rock*

If every teenager before this film didn't want jeans already, they *definitely* did now. Levi's began selling a new pair of black jeans called Elvis Presley jeans. And sales exploded.

At the 1980 Winter Olympics in Lake Placid, New York, and again during the 1984 Games in Sarajevo, Yugoslavia, the US teams wore Levi's jeans, jackets, and cowboy hats during the opening

US athletes in Levi's at the 1980 Winter Olympics

ceremonies. They were America's team wearing America's favorite brand. Millions of people all over the world saw the all-American clothes worn by the US Olympians. Now even more people wanted to wear the Levi's brand, too.

CHAPTER 12
Levi's Today

Today, Levi's is the world's largest jean seller. The company has more than sixteen thousand employees in 110 countries, including countries in Europe and Asia. It's difficult to travel internationally and not find someone wearing a pair of Levi's jeans anywhere you go.

In 1999, *Time* magazine named the 501 jeans the fashion item of the twentieth century, and about four years later, in 2003, the company celebrated the one hundred and thirtieth anniversary of the invention of blue jeans.

In 2014, Levi's Stadium was built in the San Francisco Bay area. It became the new home field of the San Francisco 49ers. The 49ers are named

after the year of the Gold Rush, the same time Levi was beginning to build his company, and the team's mascot, Sourdough Sam, wears Levi's jeans at the games. In fact, fans are given rewards, such as free snacks, when they wear a pair of Levi's to a game, too.

Levi Strauss & Co. also continues to do philanthropic work across the country.

The Levi Strauss Foundation has donated more than $340 million to over one thousand communities all over the world. The money helps provide access to education and health care. The company also works to combat climate change, for immigrant rights, and to help stop gun violence. The foundation also helps other people start businesses of their own, just like Levi himself did so long ago.

"Giving back is at the core of our business," says Daniel Lee, executive director of the Levi Strauss

Foundation, "a pillar put in place by our founder, Levi Strauss."

The Levi Strauss & Company slogan is "Quality Never Goes Out Of Style." The man, and his contributions to the world, have not gone out of style, either. The slogan also proves that Levi's name—after all these years—is just as durable as his jeans.

Timeline of Levi Strauss's Life

1829 — Born Loeb Strauss on February 26 in Buttenheim, Bavaria

1847 — Strauss family sails to New York City

1853 — Becomes an American citizen on January 31

— Arrives in San Francisco on March 14

1866 — Levi Strauss & Co. headquarters moves to 14-16 Battery Street, where it remains for the next forty years

1873 — Levi and Jacob Davis receive a patent on May 20 for the riveted pants that will eventually be called jeans

1875 — Levi named in the *New York Times* as one of the "San Francisco Millionaires"

1880 — Levi Strauss & Co. sales reach over $2 million, with close to three hundred employees, including factory workers, salesmen, and bookkeepers

1886 — Two-horse leather patch is first used on Levi's jeans

1890 — Nephews Jacob, Sigmund, Louis, and Abraham become partners in his company

1897 — Donates funds for twenty-eight scholarships at the University of California, Berkeley, and gives money to the California School for the Deaf

1902 — Dies on September 26 at home in San Francisco at the age of seventy-three

Timeline of the World

1846	United States declares war on Mexico on May 13
1848	California Gold Rush begins
1850	California becomes a US state on September 9
1858	Minnesota becomes a US state on May 11
1860	Pony Express begins operation
1861	US Civil War begins
1865	US Civil War ends on April 9; President Abraham Lincoln is shot on April 14
1869	US Transcontinental Railroad is completed
1875	First Kentucky Derby race
1876	Alexander Graham Bell patents the telephone
1877	Race riots occur in San Francisco
1881	Construction begins on the Panama Canal
1883	Brooklyn Bridge is finished
1901	Theodore Roosevelt becomes president of the United States
1903	Orville and Wilbur Wright fly the first airplane

Bibliography

*Books for young readers

Brooks, John. "Annals of Business: A Friendly Product." *The New Yorker*, November 12, 1979.

Cray, Ed. *Levi's*. Houghton Mifflin: Boston, 1978.

Downey, Lynn. *Levi Strauss & Co.* Arcadia Publishing: Charleston, SC, 2009.

*Ford, Carin T. *Levi Strauss: The Man Behind Blue Jeans.* Enslow Publishing: Berkeley Heights, NJ, 2004.

*Henry, Sondra, and Emily Taitz. *Everyone Wears His Name: A Biography of Levi Strauss.* Dillon Press: New York, 1990.

Lewis, Oscar. *This Was San Francisco*. David McKay Company: New York, 1962.

Rochlin, Harriet, and Fred Rochlin. *Pioneer Jews: A New Life in the Far West.* Houghton Mifflin Company: Boston, 1984.

*Weidt, Maryann N. *Mr. Blue Jeans: A Story About Levi Strauss.* Millbrook Press: Minneapolis, 1990.

Websites

www.levistrauss.com

www.levi-strauss-museum.de/en/museum/